I0171562

STANDARD ON CONTRACTING FOR ASSESSMENT SERVICES

STANDARD ON CONTRACTING FOR ASSESSMENT SERVICES

Approved April 2019

International Association of Assessing Officers

IAAO assessment standards represent a consensus in the assessing profession and have been adopted by the Board of Directors of the International Association of Assessing Officers (IAAO). The objective of the IAAO standards is to provide a systematic means for assessing officers to improve and standardize the operation of their offices. IAAO standards are advisory in nature and the use of, or compliance with, such standards is voluntary. If any portion of these standards is found to be in conflict with national, state, or provincial laws, such laws shall govern. Ethical and/or professional requirements within the jurisdiction[1] may also take precedence over technical standards.

[1] For example, USPAP, CUSPAP, IVS, EVS.

About IAAO

The International Association of Assessing Officers, formerly the National Association of Assessing Officers, was founded for the purpose of establishing standards for assessment personnel. IAAO is a professional membership organization of government assessment officials and others interested in the administration of the property tax. Over the years IAAO members have developed assessment practice and administration standards and many of these standards have been adopted by state and international oversight agencies, and some have been incorporated into legislation.

IAAO continues at the forefront of assessment in North America and has been expanding its reach to the global community for the last five decades. Because standards form the rules by which North American assessors perform their duties, they may not be directly applicable to an overseas audience. The standards have been updated to also present the broad principles upon which the rules are based. IAAO believes those principles may be adapted to many differing statutory and regulatory scenarios worldwide.

Acknowledgments

At the time of the 2018 rewrite of this standard, the Task Force on Standard on Contracting for Assessment Services was composed of Carol A. Neihardt, Chair; Joe Guy, Jeff Tompkins, Bryan Williams, and Joel Moser, Esq.

Revision notes
This standard replaces the 2008 Standard on Contracting for Assessment Services and is a complete revision. The 2008 standard updated the 2002 standard.

Published by
International Association of Assessing Officers
314 W 10th St
Kansas City, Missouri 64105-1616
816-701-8100 • Fax: 816-701-8149
www.iaao.org
Library of Congress Catalog Card Number: ISBN 978-0-88329-247-1

Copyright © 2019 by the International Association of Assessing Officers All rights reserved.

No part of this publication may be reproduced in any form, in an electronic retrieval system or otherwise, with- out the prior written permission of the publisher. IAAO grants permission for copies to be made for educational use as long as (1) copies are distributed at or below cost, (2) IAAO is identified as the publisher, and (3) proper notice of the copyright is affixed.

Produced in the United States of America.

CONTENTS

1. Scope 1

2. Overview 2

3. Soliciting for Products or Services 3

    3.1 Purpose...3

    3.2 Preparation 4

    3.3 Requirements Gathering 4

    3.4 Solicitation Development 6

    3.5 Contractual and Legal Requirements 8

    3.6 Solicitation Assembly and Response Requirements 9

    3.7 Vendor Proposals and Communication 9

4. Solicitation Review 10

    4.1 Selection and Communication 10

    4.2 Legal Considerations...10

5. Contract Award 11

    5.1 Preparation..11

    5.2 Negotiation 11

    5.3 Delivery and Payment Approaches..11

    5.4 Signature 11

6. Contract and Vendor Oversight 12

    6.1 Delivery Acceptance...12

    6.2 Project Planning..12

    6.3 Communication 13

    6.4 Governance and Progress Tracking 13

    6.5 Contract Changes..14

    6.6 Delivery Assurance 14

7. Considerations by Service and Product 15

    7.1 Professional Services...15

        7.1.1 Data Collection...15

        7.1.2 Revaluations..15

        7.1.3 Consulting Services 16

    7.2 Software Design and Implementation 16

    7.3 System Hardware 17

References...18

Appendix A. Solicitation Formats..19

A.1 Request for Information 20

A.2 Invitation for Bid/Request for Bid 21

A.3 Review of Qualifications..21

A.4 Request for Proposal 22

A.5 Cooperative Purchasing (Intergovernmental Agreement or IGA Contracts................22

A.6 Selecting the Correct Format..23

STANDARD ON CONTRACTING FOR ASSESSMENT SERVICES

1. SCOPE

This standard describes and makes recommendations on the development, awarding, and monitoring of contracts for assessment services. Each major section begins with the main principles covered in that section, followed by a description of those principles.

Principles

The key principles within this standard are as follows:

- *The solicitation for contract services must clearly describe the project, including major deadlines and the means by which success will be measured.*

- *The contract for services must clearly and completely describe the project as well as the parties involved and their responsibilities.*

- *There must be a complete understanding of the methods and means for monitoring the project, including the determination of project completion.*

2. OVERVIEW

Assessment contracts are developed to provide assessment services to government agencies by firms or private individuals. Throughout this standard the government agency awarding the contract is referred to as the *assessment agency* and the firm or private individual to whom the contract is awarded as the *contractor*.

Assessment contracts can cover any services relating to the discovery, listing, appraisal, and assessment of property including data collection and mapping; development of construction cost or valuation manuals; complete or partial revaluations; specialized consulting services; tax policy matters; and system design and implementation including development of appraisal and assessment software.

3. SOLICITING FOR PRODUCTS OR SERVICES

Principles

- *Clearly and completely state the services or technology to be procured along with any delivery quality and quantity requirements.*

- *Establish a competitive environment intended to maximize the value for the department; identify only qualified solutions; and inform decision-makers of the necessary elements required to select the most qualified solution.*

- *Clearly define all response requirements, processes, and information that are required to enable the responder to meet any legal and department rules, laws, and requirements and to successfully communicate the offer.*

- *Provide decision-makers and department legal staff with as much information as possible to start the contract negotiation process.*

3.1 PURPOSE

Soliciting for products or services, at its most basic, is requesting a third party to perform services when the assessment agency does not have the time, resources, or expertise to successfully perform the required tasks. To receive optimal results from a solicitation, the assessment agency must exercise careful planning and understanding of

- The current work environment
- The separation of requirement from desires
- The scope of what the responding vendor shall deliver
- Controls over the acceptability of what is delivered.

When performed properly, a solicitation provides the assessment agency and the respondent with a clear set of uniform expectations, terms, conditions, and scope that allows for the highest level of competition from a level playing field of competing vendors.

3.2 PREPARATION

Before starting the solicitation process, the agency should identify the teams and resources necessary to support the overall goals of the solicitation. The following teams of assessment agency personnel are vital to the success of the solicitation:

- **Evaluation Team.** This team is directly responsible for the review and evaluation of vendor proposals. Under the direction of a procurement official, this team determines the factors to be utilized for evaluating proposals and respondents and is responsible for the selection of the vendor best suited to meet the requirements. Ideally, the team consists of three to five members who have sufficient professional knowledge to make an educated evaluation of the proposals.
- **Subject Matter Expert (SME).** This team has specific knowledge and/or expertise in a particular facet of the requirements. SMEs act as support to the evaluators and provide insight into scope development and proposal evaluation.
- **Executive Team (Steering Committee).** This team of managers is responsible for general project oversight and provides executive level support of the solicitation initiatives. The team may also act as the final arbiter of business change decisions.

Once these teams are assembled, it is advisable to have them disclose any potential conflict of interest with the anticipated pool of respondents. In addition, they should consent to comply with a nondisclosure agreement to ensure the integrity of the solicitation.

The final resources needed are human and financial. Human resources include additional staff members who may be necessary either to support the project or to backfill team members assigned to the team. Financial resources include the budget capacity to afford the eventual solution proposed by the vendors. Having the budget decided in advance aids in focusing the scope of the solicitation.

3.3 REQUIREMENTS GATHERING

Requirements gathering may be the most important step in the solicitation process and is vital to the success of the contract. The guiding principle of requirements gathering is asking "What else?" or "What next?" For example, if a requirement is for a stapler, the "what else/next" questions are as follows:

- How many are needed?
- When are they needed?
- Where are they needed?
- What capacity do they need to accommodate?
- What accessories or supplies are necessary?
- What happens when they break?

It is important to look beyond the basic need into all possible impacts on, and by, the requirement.

If the proposed project is the selection of customized off-the-shelf (COTS) software or the development of a specific application, a more detailed approach is necessary. Requirements should be segregated between functional and technical. Functional requirements are specific tasks the software must perform ("the solution shall assign a unique person identifier that is used to connect all related information about that person"). Technical requirements are centered on specific software architecture and ongoing support ("the solution shall protect audit log information from unauthorized access"). All requirements should be defined in one to two sentences and compiled into spreadsheets. These sheets can then be converted into a solicitation response tool in which the respondents detail how the solution complies with the requirement or identify how they will modify or configure their solution to comply.

A beneficial approach is to start with a basic list of the assumed needs of the project (either products or services). It is also advisable to have multiple SMEs develop independent lists of needs and consolidate them, as a group, to produce a priority list. The group must then determine items that are actual needs (requirements) versus those that are wants (options). Creating an overly comprehensive set of requirements may discourage some potential respondents

and limit the pool of proposals. Care should be exercised to produce a solicitation that promotes receiving the largest and most competitive group of potential vendors.

Because of the complex nature of requirements gathering, it may be useful to contract with a consulting firm to as- sist in the process. A key advantage of a consultant is having an objective third-party explore all the aspects of the requirements to help expose any gaps or assumed processes the respondent needs to know in order to provide a fully educated proposal. Consultants also may provide valuable best practices information to aid in the creation of the scope of work (SOW).

Requirements extend beyond the need for products or services because they also define the type of acceptable vendors. Respondent qualification requirements can be expressed by the following:

- Years of direct experience (individual and company)
- Years in the marketplace
- Number of similar projects in terms of scope, size, and/or complexity
- Size of the company
- Certification and licenses
- Hours of operation.

It is necessary to ensure the requirements are not overly burdensome, do not cause an undue restriction on competition, are common to the marketplace, and are not designed to preselect a given vendor. The requirements must be verifiable in an objective manner (e.g., confirming licensing from the issuing agency).

3.4 SOLICITATION DEVELOPMENT

The SOW is the narrative support of the requirements identified by the project team. The scope is the guiding document for the vendor's proposal and becomes the portion of the contract that dictates the functions of the successful contractor.

The following list outlines the content of an SOW. Depending on the complexity of the SOW, it may be necessary to augment this list with supplemental exhibits to provide more in-depth information or examples for the vendor.

- **Intent.** This is a basic statement of what the solicitation is being issued for and the type of contract to be awarded ("the county is seeking to award a single contract for the provision of property valuation services").

- **Goals and objectives.** This is generally a bullet point list of anticipated outcomes of the proposed solution.

- **Background information.** This should be used to describe both the pertinent structure and operation of the assessment agency and any processes that are going to be affected by the solution.

- **Scope narrative.** This section describes the function of the desired solution. It is important to understand the risk of over-prescribing particular actions of the contractor. If the direction is poorly communicated or structured, the contractor cannot be found in default of the agreement.

- **Requirements matrix (if applicable).** This is the refined list of functional and technical requirements organized by functional area.

- **Deliverables.** This is a list of what the contractor is expected to provide in terms of services and tangible items (reports).

- **Timeline.** The timeline outlines the desired commencement and completion dates as well as any date restrictions with an impact on the contractor's ability to perform (i.e., closure for inventory).

- **Performance standards.** Standards are highly dependent on the nature of the solicitation. For services, standards can be expressed in terms of timely performance and quality. A formal service-level agreement (SLA) should be used if the contractor will be providing a software solution. The SLA should incorporate minimum software functionality, support response times, software availability standards, and potential penalties for nonperformance.

- **Training and education.** The solicitation should identify the responsibilities of the contractor with respect to training and education of agency personnel in use of the new system, products, or services. These responsibilities should include a description of the numbers, content, and duration of any formal training sessions, instructors, materials, and training aids to be provided to the agency.

- **Public relations.** The solicitation should identify the responsibilities of the contractor with respect to public relations including public hearings and meetings, media contact, internet access, and the response to inquiries and public records information requests. Public relations are particularly important in data collection. See the Standard on Public Relations (IAAO 2011).

- **Respondent qualifications.** This can be as simple as a bullet list of minimum qualifications. This list is used to segregate contractors who do not meet the minimum standard from those who do. Those who do not can be excluded immediately.

  - *Bidders should be required to demonstrate expertise, experience, and other qualities affecting the probable success of the project.* The contractor should possess sufficient financial resources and personnel to ensure continuing commitment to the project and should be adequately insured. The agency should require and carefully review audited financial information on the contractor. References and the Federal Employee Identification Number or other required identification should be requested.

- *Acceptability and potential role of subcontractors should also be considered.* The same performance standards that apply to the primary contractor should apply to subcontractors. The primary contractor's proposal should identify the contemplated use of subcontractors and, ideally, name them and describe their qualifications and role in the project.

- *Key individuals to be assigned to the project, along with their qualifications and specific roles, should be considered.* The solicitation should specify the qualifications of the individuals who will perform the work described, because the quality of project products and services depends heavily on their expertise. The qualifications of subcontractor personnel should be specified as well. In some cases, it may be appropriate to require testing or certification of individuals assigned to the project.

- **Price model.** This describes the manner in which respondents provide price proposals. Great care should be taken to ensure the price line items are specific enough to allow for an objective comparison of proposal costs. A Total Project Cost may be acceptable; however, it is advisable to ask for a cost breakdown (labor, materials, support services, and so on). For complex projects, it is also recommended that an hourly rate be requested for a given list of job descriptions, which can be used in the event of supplemental services to the initial contract.

- **Evaluation criteria.** Evaluation criteria should be structured to evaluate the proposals as objectively as possible. The basic criteria are adherence to the scope of work/proposed approach, respondent qualification/experience (judged against minimum qualifications listed in the solicitation), and price. There are multiple tools and methodologies that can be utilized, from a straight assignment of points per category to scoring responses to a questionnaire. Regardless of tool, the key is to ensure that the evaluation is clear and defensible in the event of a solicitation or award protest.

- **Evaluation procedure.** The solicitation should explain the basis on which proposals will be evaluated and selected, including required submission dates, oral presentations, and other review and selection procedures. Some important dates include the date by which letters of intent to file a proposal must be received, the date by which proposals must be received, and the date on which proposals will be opened. The solicitation should also specify the method of packaging and labeling the proposals, so that they are not inadvertently opened before the scheduled date.

- **Additional considerations.** The assessment agency may consider adding a provision to the solicitation allowing for the opportunity to contact the next highest scored vendor in the event both parties (jurisdiction and potential vendor) cannot agree to the same terms and conditions.

3.5 CONTRACTUAL AND LEGAL REQUIREMENTS

All contracts for assessment-related services should carefully discuss the scope of the project to be performed and the obligations and rights of all parties involved. Because of the wide variation in laws and regulations, all contracts for services should be reviewed by local counsel to ensure compliance with local, state, and federal laws and procurement policies. In addition, because of the potentially complicated nature of negotiations and contract preparation, awarding of the contract should be done in conjunction with the jurisdiction's procurement office or other legal counsel. If the jurisdiction does not have a procurement office, legal counsel should always be an integral part of the contract award process.

Contracting is not an administrative task to perform lightly; great care and planning in drafting the contract is essential to ensure the project's success and to protect against a contractor's failure to perform as intended. Most commercially reasonable contracts contain detailed discussion of the following provisions:

- Description of the work to be performed, including what constitutes completion of the project
- Timeframe, delivery date, and other requirements of the project
- Definition of key legal terms
- Any conditions that must be met before the parties incur obligations to perform ("conditions precedent")
- Required representations of all parties, including professional licensure
- Process for changes of scope (both seen and unforeseen/unforeseeable), amendments, and other material modification of the project
- Rights of parties to approve in advance the assignment of legal obligations to approved subcontractors
- Amount and terms of the contract delineating all expenses (travel and other expenses), including all billable expenses
- Authorized signatures of the assessment agency and other parties
- Performance standards
- Testing standards and procedures
- Performance bonds and other insurance coverage, including indemnification, duty to defend, waivers of liability, hold harmless clauses, and warranties
- Required documentation and record retention
- Implementation, installation, and delivery dates
- Payment provisions, including the use of performance bonds or the ability of the agency to "hold back" payments until satisfaction of key milestones
- Termination rights, ability to "cure" or correct failures to perform, including "force majeure events," and compensation or penalty payments to the agency in the event of failure to perform, unavailability of funds, liquidation or bankruptcy, or other factors
- Arbitration and mediation requirements (if any) for contractual and other disputes, including payment of attorney's fees and costs incurred in a breach of performance
- Responsibilities for taxes, permits, and fees
- Requirement that all work be performed in compliance with applicable laws, statutes,

ordinances, codes, rules, and regulations, or other lawful orders of public authorities

- Notice provisions and authorized key contacts for all parties involved
- Confidentiality agreements and discussion of public records laws
- Miscellaneous drafting provisions, including without limitations statements that headings are for convenience only, entire agreement/partial invalidity statement, no third-party beneficiary rights, time calculations, good faith and fair dealing, counterparts, and survival of provisions
- Equal Opportunity and Affirmative Action, including specifying that the assessment agency is an equal opportunity and affirmative action employer and that the contractor will be required to provide an affirmative action plan or related reports as proof of nondiscrimination
- All other factors affecting the rights of the parties.

3.6 SOLICITATION ASSEMBLY AND RESPONSE REQUIREMENTS

It is typically the responsibility of a procurement professional to craft the actual solicitation document and administer the solicitation process. The key factors to be determined and communicated to the respondents are as follows:

- Solicitation date, proposal submission deadline, and proposed timeline for the evaluation process.
- The required format and content of the proposal. In order to avoid confusion and fatigue in the evaluation, respondents should be required to format their proposals in a specific order and utilize a defined naming convention so that similar sections from different proposals can be more readily compared.

3.7 VENDOR PROPOSALS AND COMMUNICATION

Once a solicitation commences, all communication by the assessment agency with current or potential vendors should cease and be directed through the procurement professional. Having a single point of communication provides

- Assurance that all potential respondents are provided with the same access to information regarding the solicitation
- Removal of the appearance of improper communication with vendors, which could result in a protest of the solicitation award.

The procurement professional should coordinate the secure receipt and distribution of the proposals to the evaluation team after the response period has been closed.

4. SOLICITATION REVIEW

Principles

- *Ensure reviews are conducted in an open and equitable manner.*
- *Reviewers should have expertise in the specific are being reviewed*
- *Reviews should be focused on providing decision support to the evaluation team.*

The submitted proposals should be evaluated based on completeness, qualifications, experience, and cost, and should address all major points covered in the solicitation. During this process, the following stages should be considered.

4.1 SELECTION AND COMMUNICATION

A designated team of individuals should be assigned as the review board for the selection process. The agency should provide the review board with an evaluation guide (checklist of items to be scored) that was drafted by the division for which the product or service is needed. This evaluation guide should be an objective scoring model with a weight per section based on relevancy, approach to completion, completion in a timely manner, and cost. The checklist should also include full verification of the potential contractor's references.

4.2 LEGAL CONSIDERATIONS

All parties and decision-making entities should carefully review the contract, obtain legal guidance and review, and sign only when fully satisfied that the contract adequately addresses the project as contemplated. The contract must stand on its own; verbal agreements and understandings should be completely avoided. Finally, multiple contracts, such as those used as part of a large project like a revaluation, require that the agency have special skills in project coordination and management and should be executed only with great care and planning.

5. CONTRACT AWARD

Principles

- *Include a comprehensive statement/SOW as needed to describe all required services and products, including quality and acceptance requirements necessary for the contractor to receive full payment. This should include department/agency responsibilities, assumptions, and requirements.*

- *Clearly state the requirements and goals for contract completion or final acceptance of all services and products.*

- *Address the relationship between the multiple contracts that may be required to fully acquire the services.*

5.1 PREPARATION

Once the evaluation team has evaluated all proposals and identified the highest scoring proposal, the assessment agency should prepare an Intent to Award to notify the vendor in writing. This award notification begins the contract process. The assessment agency should then engage the legal departments on how the contracting process is to proceed. The agency may wish to create and draft the contract based on the solicitation or standard agency framework. Depending on the documentation needed, the agency may need to work with the selected vendor to determine whether any special language is required by the vendor(s).

5.2 NEGOTIATION

The assessment agency should schedule discussions based on scope, timeline, and pricing needs that may have to be addressed differently than may have been outlined by the vendor within the solicitation response.

5.3 DELIVERY AND PAYMENT APPROACHES

It is very important that the contract clearly outline the deliverables and the payment process for each stage of the contract. The assessment agency may not want to commit to paying in full for a product or service until it has been satisfactorily delivered and tested for completion.

5.4 SIGNATURE

Signatures by both agency and vendor should be required.

6. CONTRACT AND VENDOR OVERSIGHT

Principles

- *Ensure alignment of the project plan with the objectives and intended benefits to support the achievement of the organization's goals.*
- *Provide a framework to monitor the project's scope, scheduling, and risk.*
- *Offer a complete understanding of the methods and means for monitoring the project, including the determination of project completion.*

6.1 DELIVERY ACCEPTANCE

The concept and process of work effort acceptance is an important part of any agreement with a service provider. It informs the vendor that it has completed the work, signals progress or completion of the vendor's effort, and defines the assessment agency's approval of the work.

Where possible, acceptance should be defined in advance during the contracting process for each deliverable, phase/ gate, or milestone produced by the vendor. If advance definition of acceptance is not possible, then the contract should contain criteria that produces mutually agreed-upon acceptance language. Acceptance may be defined for the entire contract or project.

Acceptance is best employed when it clearly defines, in measurable or clearly observable terms, an end state desired prior to the assessment agency taking possession of a given deliverable. Reference to project, activity, or task objectives is often vital in properly describing the criteria used to define acceptance. The process used to achieve acceptance should be defined and include any communications, forms, or other artifacts required to both initiate and conclude the acceptance being discussed.

6.2 PROJECT PLANNING

Planning is critical to successful delivery by the vendor and to minimal resource and business impacts on the organization. Collaboration with the vendor is essential to a successful project plan and should be performed to the extent practical prior to contract signing. Although a complete contract or project plan is desired, if circumstances exist that limit the ability to fully plan the project, focus on near-term activities (e.g., the first 25 percent of the project) to sup- port early success and to allow for the time to more adequately plan future activities.

Planning should encompass the following typical project phases:

- Initiation
- Definition/plan
- Execution
- Monitoring/control
- Closure.

For each project phase, consider the following elements:

- **Goals/objectives/description.** Decide what must be accomplished in that phase and the quality level to which it must be accomplished. This leads directly to acceptance criteria and the activities and tasks required to accomplish the goals.

- **Activities/tasks.** Identify the specific work and any sequencing or dependencies that must be accomplished. Consider what type of resources and skills are needed to complete the work.

- **Deliverables.** Define specific deliverables and their acceptance criteria. Include physical (documents, hardware) and less intangible (knowledge, effort, concepts) deliverables.

- **Responsibilities.** Document which party is responsible for accomplishing each defined task. Include the need for logistics, information technology, third-party, intellectual, special skills, and any other requirements needed to accomplish the work successfully.

- **Risk.** To the extent practicable, understand the risks associated with each task and phase of the project, and design tasks that may help mitigate the risk.

- **Timeline.** Estimate the duration and effort needed to accomplish each task, and construct a project schedule (timeline) accordingly. Most experienced project managers advise that slack or contingency time be factored in to accommodate unforeseen events and additional work.

6.3 COMMUNICATION

The frequent, honest, and free flow of information between the jurisdiction and the vendor is critical to success. Exchange of good and bad news, in real time, encourages truthful information exchange. To help facilitate effective project communication, consider the following.

- Written status reports
- Project Manager and status meetings
- Tracking of project commitments, decisions, and all but the most minor changes
- Specifications, test results, measurements, data, and the like that communicate interim or final outcomes
- Periodic senior-level or other stakeholder communication.

6.4 GOVERNANCE AND PROGRESS TRACKING

Project control is important for the stakeholders of both the government agency and the contractor. Having control can help the project manager/program manager compare actual performance against planned performance. The project manager can identify potential problems, evaluate alternative actions, and plan for appropriate corrective action.

Project leaders typically create a project plan that includes the tasks to be performed, the project timeline, a budget, and project resources. By monitoring the plan and the actual work performed, the project manager can measure both qualitative and quantitative progress.

If the project is deviating from the project timeline, corrective action may be necessary. Deviations can be caused by a number of issues such as change in the project scope or project resources or other setbacks. The corrective plan should be created with input from all project stakeholders.

6.5 CONTRACT CHANGES

Change control management and coping with the associated risk is a challenge for project managers. Changes can occur for a number of reasons including increase or decrease in scope and project personnel or other resource changes. The overall project plan should define project changes so that both the government agency and contractor are aware of the process required to alert and plan for them.

Change control systems involve reporting, controlling, and recording changes to the project baseline. Most change control plans include, at a minimum, identification of the proposed change, expected effects on the project, and negotiation of changes in time and budget.

6.6 DELIVERY ASSURANCE

Assessment agencies can ensure the quality of the delivery by carefully monitoring the project and by not committing to full payment for a product or service until it has been satisfactorily delivered and tested. Two ways of contractually holding a contractor responsible for delivery are a *holdback* and a *performance bond*. In a holdback provision, a specified percentage of the contract amount is withheld until the final approval and sign-off have taken place. In a performance bond, a third party, in effect, *insures* the contractor's performance. In some cases, it may be appropriate to require a performance bond of up to 100 percent of the amount of the contract. One method usually suffices.

If a contract is amended, the addendum should reference the original contract and clearly designate the new provisions or modifications.

7. CONSIDERATIONS BY SERVICE AND PRODUCT

7.1 PROFESSIONAL SERVICES

Professional services can fall into multiple categories such as consulting services or appraisal services including revaluations.

7.1.1 Data Collection
Collection of property characteristics data may be part of a contract for implementation of a mass appraisal system, or it may be contracted for separately. Data collection (or reverification) is a critical and expensive phase of any appraisal project. Clear and standard coding and careful monitoring through quality control measures ensure the quality and validity of data characteristics. The contractor may develop and use a data collection manual to achieve uniformity in data collection.

The solicitation should specify the types and approximate number of parcels involved in the project, property characteristics to be examined and codified, standards for data capture and coding accuracy, and procedures for measuring achievement of accuracy standards. It should also specify the method of data collection.

Collection of data may be done manually via an on-site inspection or electronically via aerial, orthogonal photography and change detection software. Both methods should follow data accuracy standards set by the assessment agency. Additional information regarding accuracy standards is available in the *IAAO Standard on Mass Appraisal of Real Property* (IAAO 2017).

In some cases, the assessment agency has a current file of property characteristics, and the solicitation should specify the extent to which the contractor may rely on this file. The solicitation should specify whether the contractor should use data collection forms, manuals, and coding procedures supplied by the assessment agency or whether new ones are to be developed. The qualifications of data collectors should also be set forth in the solicitation. The solicitation should indicate whether interior inspections are required and, if so, the actions to be taken when property owners are away or refuse entry. The minimum number of properties to be entered should be stated.

The assessment agency and contractor should establish quality control procedures to ensure accuracy standards are attained. The agency can address these in the solicitation or request bidders to address them in their response to the solicitation. In any case, the assessment agency should carefully monitor compliance with such standards and procedures. Good quality control procedures include sample audits (particularly at the start of the project), computerized edits for reasonableness and consistency of data, and pilot-testing of mass appraisal models using the new data.

7.1.2 Revaluations
A solicitation for revaluation services should carefully set forth the scope of the project. A revaluation project can include such major tasks as data collection, development of forms, mapping and geographic information system (GIS) development, valuation models, development of appraisal manuals, development of software, training, public relations, and defense of assessment appeals. These tasks should be described in sufficient detail to clarify the agency's requirements and performance standards for potential bidders.

The quality of a revaluation is most often measured by a ratio study. The contractor and client should agree to the design for the ratio study, if used as a measure of the quality of values produced. The design should specify the rules and procedures for sales confirmation, sales validation, adjustments to sale prices, time trending, trimming of outliers, and use of confidence levels. The design should also specify the nature of the sample used to test the revaluation. The sample should provide assurance of similar impacts on sold and unsold properties. Jurisdictional requirements for the period from which the test sample will be drawn should be considered.

If a ratio study is not used as the measure of the project's success, other methods of determining the value of the project should be outlined in the SOW.

7.1.3 Consulting Services

A solicitation, or a contract for specialized consulting services (such as auditing, ratio studies, modeling, appeal assistance including expert witness testimony, appraisal of special properties and tangible personal property, and management and performance reviews), should address the definition and scope of the task, statutory or regulatory agency requirements, adherence to the *Uniform Standards of Professional Appraisal Practice (USPAP)* (TAF 2018) or other governing agencies, the timeline, confidentiality requirements and agreements, performance standards, contract dispute resolution, ownership of the product, payment schedules, and contract start and termination dates.

7.2 SOFTWARE DESIGN AND IMPLEMENTATION

A solicitation and a contract for appraisal software system design and implementation are primarily concerned with software specifications and should set forth performance requirements in reference to existing procedures and desired results. Software in this context may be intended for, but not limited to, property appraisal, property taxation, GIS, aerial and orthogonal images, or change detection. Items that need to be addressed include hardware constraints, report- writing capabilities, legal requirements, program requirements, programming language, transferability, maintenance and updates, program support and documentation, license, copyright, and training. It is also important to clarify the ownership of the developed software, including the source code and data generated.

System documentation should be considered and addressed in the contract. User documentation relates to manuals and other instructional materials that explain proper use and operation of the system, including such items as completion of forms, classification and grading of buildings, valuation procedures, and interpretation of reports. System administration documentation relates to data processing manuals and instructions that are required by local system analysts to understand, maintain, and modify any computer programs provided under the contract. The agreement should specify the type of documentation (such as flowcharts, data definitions, and formulas) required by the jurisdiction. The solicitation should require the source code (computer programs) be either provided to the assessment agency, while giving appropriate copyright protection to the vendor, or placed in escrow with a neutral third party in the event of a contract dispute or the inability of the vendor to service the software. The solicitation should describe all service contract obligations on the part of the contractor to maintain and modify the software once installed, including modifications to comply with statutory and legal changes. The contract should establish the criteria for deciding when such modifications are complex enough to warrant additional charges beyond the basic contractual service obligations. The contract should also specify who makes that decision and the timing of such modifications.

7.3 SYSTEM HARDWARE

A solicitation and contract for electronic hardware should specify equipment compatible with the operating system and application to be installed and the needs of the assessment agency. The technical platform requirements typically specify the requirements for the application server or servers in terms of processor speed, memory, and storage. Con- sideration should also be given to the end-user equipment.

Interface requirements define at a high level how the application hardware will be integrated with other production systems used by the assessment agency. Considerations should include

- Platform
- Architecture
- Volumetric information, size of database or databases
- Ongoing interfaces.

The solicitation and contract requirements should take into account potential customization of installed software to protect the integrity of the system and ensure compatibility with future releases of the software.

Definition of security requirements, including backup and recovery concerns in relation to the assessment agency's security standards, should be considered to ensure the safety of the agency's overall electronic network.

REFERENCES

IAAO. 2011. *Standard on Public Relations.* Kansas City, MO: IAAO.

IAAO. 2017. *Standard on Mass Appraisal of Real Property.* Kansas City, MO: IAAO.

The Appraisal Foundation (TAF). 2018. *Uniform Standards of Professional Appraisal Practice (USPAP), 2018–2019* ed. Washington, DC: TAF.

APPENDIX

APPENDIX A. Solicitation Formats

The following are recommendations on available solicitation formats, development, and use. It is suggested that jurisdictions seek the advice of local governing procurement authorities and legal counsel to determine how state laws, local ordinances, and codes will affect the processes.

There are five main formats available for soliciting service:

- Request for Information (RFI)
- Invitation for Bid/Request for Bid (IFB)
- Review of Qualifications (ROQ)
- Request for Proposal (RFP)
- Cooperative Purchasing (Intergovernmental Agreements of IGA Contracts).

The following sections describe the uses, advantages, and disadvantages of each of these formats.

A.1 REQUEST FOR INFORMATION

This is the simplest of all solicitation methods. The basic function of an RFI is to request a high-level overview proposal for the requirements.

Use
An RFI is typically used when an assessment agency has insufficient knowledge of available solutions, products or services or availability of the requirements in the marketplace.

Advantages
- It does not require a fully formed SOW. Rather, it relies on a high-level statement of intent and general performance goals.
- It provides the requester with a broad base of options to understand its own requirements.
- It allows the requester to perform some measures of follow-up with the respondent in the form of questions, demonstrations, or presentations.
- It identifies viable marketplaces from which to complete a formal solicitation.

Disadvantages
- Responses typically do not include pricing and therefore do not provide budgetary information.
- A contract cannot be formed from an RFI response. The assessment agency must take the information provided from the respondents and utilize it to refine the requirements and develop a formal solicitation.
- It may not be feasible for smaller jurisdictions.

A.2 INVITATION FOR BID/REQUEST FOR BID

An IFB is the least complex of formal solicitations. Fundamentally, it is a request for a set of services at a bid-upon rate of payment (either lump sum, time and materials, or hourly).

Use
IFBs are utilized for short-term or limited-scope projects, typically on an hourly basis. The primary function is the acquisition of temporary staff.

Advantages
- An IFB is typically a quick process. Most jurisdictions do not allow for negotiation of terms or conditions on the resulting contract; this means the lowest cost respondent who meets the requirements of the solicitation is awarded the contract as is.
- It allows for specific dictation of what and how the work is to be performed.

Disadvantages
- The risk of unsuccessful outcomes rests more heavily on the assessment agency because it is responsible for dictating how and where the work is to be performed. If that direction is flawed, it is the sole fault of the assessment agency in terms of time loss and expense to mediate the flaw.
- The assessment agency must have a clear and concise understanding of the required services so they can be expressed in a few commoditized line items.
- In general, the assessment agency cannot select the respondent with higher qualifications if that respondent is not also the lowest cost respondent.

A.3 REVIEW OF QUALIFICATIONS

An ROQ is a type of award based on respondents meeting stated minimum qualifications.

Uses
An ROQ is generally used to obtain a pool of qualified vendors to perform broadly defined professional services.

Advantages
- The solicitation process is generally brief.
- It allows the assessment agency to identify a prequalified pool of vendors who can then be given specific tasks without the need of a new formal solicitation.
- It allows for a set maximum allowable charges for the service group.

Disadvantages
- The assessment agency assumes a higher responsibility for directing contractor work.
- Price flexibility and the ability to negotiate are limited.
- It is not suited for complex work in which the agency is reliant on the expertise of the contractor to develop a solution.

A.4 REQUEST FOR PROPOSAL

An RFP is the most formal of the solicitation processes in that it requires the highest level of effort to create and to evaluate. The main difference between an RFP and other solicitation types is that the respondent is required to develop a proposal for services that will meet a defined set of requirements rather than a contractor performing the requirements as directed.

Uses

An RFP can be used to select a vendor to perform large-scale services or to acquire and implement software solutions.

Advantages

- It allows for a high level of scrutiny into the vendor proposal, qualifications, past performance, product, and pricing.
- It can provide the flexibility to redline requirements during negotiation based on refined understanding of the requirements or fiscal restrictions.
- The responsibility of performance and success rests more heavily on the contractor.

Disadvantages

- A high level of discipline is required to properly identify and define requirements.
- An RFP can be a time-consuming process. A typical RFP can take 120 days from solicitation release to contract award.
- It requires expertise to evaluate proposals and to negotiate an enforceable, mutually beneficial contract.

A.5 COOPERATIVE PURCHASING (INTERGOVERNMENTAL AGREEMENTS OR IGA CONTRACTS)

Cooperative purchasing is defined as either the utilization of another government entity's competitively solicited con-

tract for the acquisition of goods or services or the combining of requirements of two or more government entities to collectively solicit. If the jurisdiction allows for it, the procurement authority inherent in another party's solicitation and award can be used as justification for not issuing an individual entity's solicitation and negotiating an independent contract with that awarded vendor.

Advantages

- The contracts are available for immediate use.
- IGA contracts require limited expertise and resources to evaluate the appropriateness of the contract for the stated need.

Disadvantages

- The awarding agency may not have similar volumes of purchase as the assessment agency; this may result in a loss of economy of scale.
- The awarding agency may require a usage fee for the contract.
- If there are disagreements with the contractor, there may not be any direct contractual

remedy for nonperformance.

- If there are contractual disagreements, remedies may be limited.
- There may not be any direct contractual remedy for contractor nonperformance.

A.6 SELECTING THE CORRECT FORMAT

There are multiple formats for soliciting and selecting vendors. A simple way to select the correct format is to deter- mine the most important factors for selecting a contract. Table A-1 correlates the primary selection factor with the appropriate format.

TABLE A-1. Format for selection factor	
Primary Selection Factor	**Recommended Format**
Price	IFB
Qualifications	ROQ
Methodology and approach	RFP
Expediency	IGA

ASSESSMENT STANDARDS OF THE INTERNATIONAL ASSOCIATION OF ASSESSING OFFICERS

Guide to Assessment Standards

Standard on Assessment Appeal

Standard on Automated Valuation Models

Standard on Contracting for Assessment Services

Standard on Data Quality

Standard on Digital Cadastral Maps and Parcel Identifiers

Standard on Manual Cadastral Maps and Parcel Identifiers

Standard on Mass Appraisal of Real Property

Standard on Oversight Agency Responsibilities

Standard on Professional Development

Standard on Property Tax Policy

Standard on Public Relations

Standard on Ratio Studies

Standard on Valuation of Personal Property

Standard on Valuation of Property Affected by Environmental Contamination

Standard on Verification and Adjustment of Sales

TO DOWNLOAD THE CURRENT APPROVED VERSION OF ANY OF THE STANDARDS LISTED ABOVE, VISIT IAAO.ORG

www.ingramcontent.com/pod-product-compliance
Lightning Source LLC
Chambersburg PA
CBHW081644040426
42449CB00015B/3456